Publication authorised by

Consorzio per la Tutela del Palio di Siena

SIENA

Distributed by
Fabio Turbanti
Via B. Tolomei 9 - Tel. 0577 - 51260
SIENA

Centro Stampa Editoriale

plurigraf

Perseus

SIENA

"Cor Magis Tibi Sena Pandit" (Siena opens her heart out to you much wider than this door!). These words are written on the front of Porta Camollia , which is the Northernmost and also most important of the Sienese gates. This well-wishing Sienese embrace, which greeted foreigners to the city a long time ago, still welcomes tourists of today, all going to show the hospitable nature of Siena and the Sienese.

Siena and the Sienese: in very few parts of the world will one find a truer and more authentic union; a city made to measure for its people who, in turn, jealously watch over their own city, proudly and wisely maintaining its institutions and monuments as well as preserving the memory of its past.

As a matter of fact, although the city has been through many stormy events - namely sieges, civil struggles and political disturbances - seen each and every kind of disaster and witnessed the highest heroic acts, in spite of all this it has managed to preserve intact its original appearance of a medieval city, its own history and monuments.

The tourist who goes along the modern road leading to Siena from Florence; sees all around himself a very pleasant landscape, rich in green fields of olive-trees, vineyards and cypresses. The medieval and characteristic towers of S. Gimignano rising on the right side, near Poggibonsi, tell us that Siena is near.

The landscape looks quite different to those who reach the town through the south of the province by the Cassia or Valdichiana roads. This side of the country, though bare in some of its parts, presents characteristic and suggestive features, thanks mainly to its picturesque clays and hills of clay with their corn-fields. On top of these hills there is always a tree, as if it were a sort of plume. Siena was a Roman colony during the Republican age. During the imperial age and the early Middle Ages, it went through many terrible events. Its expansion, however, was always limited by the greater power and rivalry of Florence. Being far from the sea and open only towards the lands of the Maremma, Siena was often besieged and devastated and had to face civil wars and terrible pestilences. After the domination of the Longobards and Franks, it passed under the Bishop-Counts, towards the middle of the 11th century. Then there was the turn of the Consuls, with a lay government. And it was in this period that Siena reached the height of its political and economic power, specially after the famous battle of Montaperti in 1260, by which it defeated the Florentines. Arts and culture flourished in this time. Thanks mainly to the Government of the Nine, which, restored in 1277, ruled for about 70 years, the magnificent monuments of Siena were built during this period of time. The renowned "Piazza del Campo" is its most precious pearl and the centre of its peculiar town-planning.

Aerial view of Piazza del Campo.

View from above of the Cathedral.

This square, with its famous buildings, is the spacious and resounding shell, where the city-life takes place.

It is the suggestive amphitheatre, whose back-ground is constituted only by the "Palazzo Pubblico" with the Tower of Mangia, the best example of 14th century civil architecture. The characteristic medieval look of Siena dates back to the same century.

The town has kept its original look. In its streets made of bricks and stones, among the high buildings, adorned with elegant three-mullioned windows and slender ogive arches, in the suggestive courtyards, in the closed and dark entrance halls, in the narrow alleys and squares, you perceive a sort of ancient atmosphere, which makes Siena so charming.

It is a medieval town, but mostly a town of art. If one is intensely excited at the sight of the Campo, one is amazed at the sight of the monuments of the town, the Cathedral and the other churches, the museums. Everywhere one finds precious masterpieces, wonderful works by Nicola and Giovanni Pisano, Duccio and Simone Martini, Donatello and Ghiberti, who have left here some examples of their immortal art.

Painting, which was the most genuine and significant expression of the creativeness of the Sienese, new architectonic ideas and an original school of sculpture, one of the best in Italy, more refined technics in gold working and designs, made of Siena one of the greatest leaders in the field of art in Italy and Europe, since the end of the 13th century and the early 14th century.

If in the 14th century Sienese art reached its height with Duccio and Simone Martini, Pietro and Ambrogio Lorenzetti, we must not forget that during the two next centuries the figurative arts reached very high levels, thanks to artists like Jacopo della Quercia, Sassetta, Sano di Pietro, Giovanni di Paolo, just to mention a few. When in the 17th century the Town of Siena declined because of internal divisions and the decreasing richness of its merchants and bankers and so was overcome by the rising power of Florence and annexed to the Grand Duchy of Tuscany, its people took refuge, as it were, in the glories of the past, in its institutions and greatest memories.

Being conscious of having a personality of their own, the Sienese people kept its love for the old districts, its civil and religious traditions, the Palio, which is something more than a horse-race. The Palio is a wonderful show commemorating the glory of the ancient Republic. It is a popular feast, which, since the Middle Ages, aroused people's enthusiasm. By the Palio, the Sienese express the feelings and passions of their 17 "contrade" or districts. And it is by this fight among the contrade that ancient Siena goes on living together with the actual Siena, in the harmonious and suggestive atmosphere of an historical and artistic environment, which is unique in the world.

The Majesty by Duccio di Buoninsegna.

PIAZZA DEL CAMPO

Piazza del Campo is Siena's main "square". Its unique shape, the splendid buildings which overlook it and the events which it hosts make it one of the most interesting and lively squares in the whole world.

It stands at the meeting point of the three hills on which the city lies. The need to transform this desolate and irregular tract of land arose in the 12th century, when it was decided to regulate the rainwater along the sloping land by implementing a system of canals. The result was a marvellous blend of nature and human genius. The Campo is laid out in the form of a shell, paved with brick in a herring-bone pattern and subdivided into nine sections. Grey stone slabs form a border all the way around.

The brick paving dates back to 1347: the nine divisions recall the Government of Nine, an oligarchy of rich merchants and bankers who led Siena to great prosperity, evidence of which can still be seen today in the most important city monuments built in that period. The elegant fourteenth century buildings which enhance the square also reflect that period of the city's splendour. One such example is **Palazzo Sansedoni** with its refined façade studded with pointed three-mullioned windows and its superb tower, which at one time competed in terms of height with that of the Palazzo Pubblico in front, whose architectural features it expressly recalls. Begun in 1216, the palazzo underwent a series of works to embellish and enlarge

A view of the atmospheric Piazza del Campo.

it in the second half of the fourteenth century. Next-door is the **Chigi-Zondadori** palace, a very ancient building whose present-day eighteenth century aspect should be attributed to Antonio Valeri. Almost at the centre of the semi-circle of the Campo, stands the elegant **Gaia Fountain**, constructed between 1409 and 1419 by Jacopo della Quercia. Built in place of another fountain, constructed in the fourteenth century, this work by the Tuscan artist anticipates in an extraordinary way some of the features which were to develop in the Renaissance period. The white sculptures representing the *Madonna* surrounded by the *Virtues*, the *Creation of Adam* and the *Expulsion from the Garden of Eden* are integrated into a specific architectural context. The suppleness of the curves and reliefs, the fullness of the sculpted forms and the delicacy of the decorations are all remarkable. The original reliefs are now housed in the Loggia of the Palazzo Pubblico, the ones displayed here being the nineteenth century reproductions by Tito Sarocchi.

The Gaia Fountain and the Acca Laurentia statue with Romulus and Remus.

PALAZZO PUBBLICO

At the bottom end of the Campo looms the outline of the magnificent **Palazzo Pubblico** with the Torre del Mangia towering above, at the foot of which stands the Piazza Chapel.

Begun after 1250 and finished in 1310, it was at one time the seat of the Podestà and the ancient Sienese Republic; nowadays the building is used as the municipal headquarters and is one of the best-known Gothic constructions in the whole of Tuscany, distinguished by its famous Sienese arches. This is a *leitmotiv* which we shall find in many of the civil buildings in the town:

The Palazzo Pubblico with the magnificent Torre del Mangia.

consisting of three-mullioned windows framed by full Gothic arches, the latter being decorated with slender white marble columns and, in this case, with the coat of arms of the city.

The lower part of the façade is made of stone, while the second and third storeys are brick with two orders of arches. The fourth storey, which is elevated with respect to the two main side parts of the building, is surmounted by a crown of small arches and merlons, which also run along the top of the third floor. The raised storey dates back to the end of the 1600s.

The **Torre del Mangia**, which, if its lightning conductor is also taken into account, is 102 metres high, looks out over the whole of Siena and is a masterpiece of the engineering of the age.

So-called after the nickname given to its bell-ringer, Giovanni di Duccio, known as the Man-giaguadagni (profit-eater), or Mangia (eater) for short, it consists of a high brick building with a belfry designed by Lippo Memmi. The bell (1655) is known as the Campanone or Sunto, in memory of the blessed name of Our Lady of the Assumption.

The **Cappella di Piazza** in white marble, is made up of pillars decorated with statues, including those of Saint John the Baptist by Lando di Stefano and Saint Thomas by Giovanni di Turino. The parapets at the entrance are decorated with bas-reliefs belonging to another 13th century monument and were partially reconstructed by Andrea Becheroni in 1846. The altar is decorated with a *Madonna with Saints and the Eternal* by Sodoma. Inside the Palazzo is the **Courtyard of the Podestà** dating back to 1325. The rooms on the upper floors of the Palazzo are now used to house the **Civic Museum**.

Palazzo Pubblico: Hall of the Globe, the Majesty - Simone Martini.

Top: Hall of the Globe, *Guidoriccio da Fogliano - Simone Martini.*
Bottom: Peace Hall, *Effects of Good Government - Ambrogio Lorenzetti.*

Top: Palazzo Pubblico Chapel.
Bottom: Hall of Pillars - Saint Bernardino's sermon in the Campo -Neroccio di Bartolomeo Landi.

On the walls of the **Hall of the Globe** we can see respectively the *Majesty* and *Guidoriccio da Fogliano* by Simone Martini.

The **Peace Hall** or the **Hall of Nine** houses the best known frescos with a civil subject to have come out of the entire mediaeval period: the *Allegories of Good and Bad Government* by Ambrogio Lorenzetti. In the **Palazzo Pubblico Chapel**, the panel by Sodoma depicting the *Holy Family and Saint Leonard* is worthy of mention.

In the **Hall of Pillars** opposite the Peace Hall are two priceless compartments of a predella depicting *San Bernardino's sermon in the Campo*, by Neroccio di Bartolomeo Landi.

PALAZZO SANSEDONI

This building, with its great size, its tower which was once even higher and more magnificent, and its curved form in line with the shape of the Piazza del Campo, resembles very closely the Palazzo Pubblico. Its series of elegant three-mullioned windows blends equally harmoniously into the overall architectural complex of the square. The construction of the building dates back to 1216; however, in 1339 it was extended and converted under the direction of Agostino di Giovanni.

Palazzo Sansedoni in Piazza del Campo.

THE CATHEDRAL

Siena Cathedral is an important point of reference for the whole of Italian Gothic architecture. Begun towards 1230, it provided a basic model for a cathedral and was subsequently adopted in many other cities. The lower Romanesque **façade** is due to Giovanni Pisano (1284) and consists of three large portals decorated with statues also by Pisano, the originals of which are housed in the Cathedral Museum. The upper part, in the flamboyant Gothic style, was finished towards the end of the fourteenth century by Giovanni di Cecco. The three cusps are now covered with mosaics by Augusto Castellani (1877).

The building works of this religious complex were constantly

An overall view of Siena Cathedral.

Interior of the Cathedral

Interior of the Cathedral - Floor.

and in the transepts, including the **Chapel of the Madonna of the Vow**, commissioned by Pope Alexander VI in 1661 and built to a design by Bernini, where we find several statues also by Bernini and by some of his pupils. Another fine **Chapel** is that of **Saint John the Baptist** dating back to 1482. In the central niche is a powerful bronze statue of the Baptist, a late work by Donatello, while the surrounding frescos were executed by Pinturicchio between 1501 and 1504. Worthy of note is the magnificent marble decoration of the **floor** which is completely storiated with graffito decoration and marquetry. Fifty-six pictures with a biblical or historical subject are depicted, executed between 1300 and 1500 by illustrious artists, including Matteo di Giovanni, who is responsible for the *Slaughter of the Innocents*.

The **High Altar** is the result of a project by Baldassarre Peruzzi, while the **wooden choir** dating from the end of the 1300s is the work of various carvers including Francesco and Jacopo del Tonghio. The central Renaissance stalls, designed by Riccio, were added in the second half of the 1500s. Another fine altar in the left-hand nave is the **Piccolomini Altar**, commissioned in 1481 by Cardinal Francesco Piccolomini. Of interest are the 4 statues standing in the niches: they were sculpted by Michelangelo between 1501 and 1504 and depict respectively Saint Paul and Saint Peter above; Saint Gregory and Saint Pius below. The hexagonal **Dome**, erected between 1259 and 1264, is supported by six pillars. It is decorated with gilded statues of saints by Ventura Turapilli and Bastiano di Francesco. A series of niches at the top contains the portraits of 42 patriarchs and prophets.

being interrupted for a variety of reasons, such as lack of funds or the plague of 1348. As a result, the magnificent project which had intended to place a much larger building alongside the one already existing was soon abandoned. All that remains of that dream are several of the front perimeter walls, the right-hand side nave and the wall of the façade. The present-day church is built to a Latin cross design, with a hexagon at the junction of the arms covered by a lanterned dome. The majestic effect of its three-naved **interior** is accentuated by the black and white striped marble decoration of the walls and columns. A number of chapels are housed along the side naves

THE CATHEDRAL PULPIT

The Cathedral **Pulpit** was executed by Nicola Pisano between 1266 and 1268 and is one of the most distinguished works in the whole of Italian sculpture.

Its spatial isolation with respect to the walls and the columns makes it fully self-sufficient in architectural terms. The pulpit is hexagonal in design; it rises up on columns alternately supported by lions (the central one at the bottom shows, for the first time in a religious decoration, the Liberal Arts and Philosophy). The capitals of the columns are surmounted by small trilobed arches with figures of the Evangelists and prophets and the Virtues on each of the corner edges.

The gallery is made up of 5 rectangular storiated panels, separated by holy figures: The Madonna and Child, Christ the Judge, Christ with the emblems of the Apocalypse, the Tetramorph, the Doctors of the Church and The Angels of the Judgement. The depictions on the faces include The Slaughter of the Innocents, as well as the Nativity, the Adoration of the Magi, the Crucifixion and The Last Judgment.

There are obvious Gothic influences from beyond the Alps. The depiction of The Nativity is unusual: instead of the classical triptych Madonna-Child-Saint Joseph, we have the Madonna showing the Child to Saint Elizabeth. The Presentation at the Temple is joined by the Flight into Egypt. There are two panels for the Last Judgement to allow for the teeming great mass of bodies: on one side are the Chosen, enraptured in beatific ecstasy and on the other the Reprobates in tears and desperation as they are driven towards eternal punishment. Pisano's collaborators were Arnolfo di Cambio and his son Giovanni.

The Pulpit by Nicola Pisano.

HOSPITAL OF SANTA MARIA DELLA SCALA

Opposite the Cathedral steps stands the hospital building of Santa Maria della Scala, the oldest in Europe. It certainly dates back to the 12th century, although it has been dated by some to around the 9th century. The façade of the building is fairly composite with the lower part covered partly in white marble and partly in brick with typical pointed portals in the Sienese style. The central floor is studded with typical double lancet windows set in blind Gothic arches, with the exception of the part above the two main doors. The interior is decorated with a series of particularly interesting frescos depicting customs of the age, such as the caring of the poor and the sick. Inside the former hospital we can now admire the **Pilgrim's Hall** with interesting frescos by Domenico di Bartolo as-

sisted by Vecchietta, which illustrate the story and the life of the building. Among the other rooms worthy of mention is the **Old Sacristy**, with paintings by Vecchietta. The **Siena Archaeological Museum** is also housed here and contains both public and private archaeological finds from the environs of Siena and Chiusi, which were excavated between the end of the nineteenth century and the first decades of the present century. Adjacent to the Hospital is the **Church of the SS. Annunziata**, built in 1252 and adapted in 1465. The single-naved church has a raised presbytery, an elegant wooden choir and a fine statue of the *Risen Christ* (1476) by Vecchietta. The fresco in the apse, depicting the sacrificial basin in front of the Temple in Jerusalem, is dated 1732 and is the work of Sebastiano Conca.

Hospital of Santa Maria della Scala: interior of the Church of the SS. Annunziata.

View of the Cathedral.

CATHEDRAL MUSEUM

Of the part of the New Cathedral which is still standing, the first three arches in the right-hand nave have survived and have been used to house the Cathedral Museum. It is here that many of the works of art specially created for the interior of the Cathedral are to be found, both to improve the conditions necessary for their preservation and as a result of the substitutions which have taken place over the years. There are priceless pieces which range from groups of sculptures and paintings to wooden, terracotta and bronze objects, as well as precious miniatures and objects wrought by goldsmiths, making this one of the most important museums in Italy. On the **ground floor** in a spacious room divided by a large fourteenth century gate in wrought iron, are the ten statues which Giovanni Pisano had sculpted for the façade of the Cathedral, including the *Mary of Moses*, in which the strong Gothic influence from beyond the Alps is particularly noticeable. *Abacuc, Moses, the Sibyl and Isaiah* reveal an intensely dramatic plastic quality which places Giovanni Pisano among the greats of European Gothic sculpture.

In the centre of the room is the high-relief by Jacopo della Quercia, depicting *The Madonna and Child, Saint Anthony the Abbot and Cardinal Antonio Casini kneeling*, a work by the mature artist which is very close to the style of Donatello. On the **first floor** in the **Duccio Room** is an absolute masterpiece: the *Majesty* by Duccio di Buoninsegna, the magnificent altarpiece which provides

---

Cathedral Museum: lower room.

20

Stories of the Passion of Christ - Duccio di Buoninsegna.

an important point of reference for the flourishing fourteenth century period of Sienese painting. In 1308 the Sienese Cathedral Construction Board commissioned from Duccio an altarpiece for the high altar depicting the Majesty of the Madonna. Finished in 1311, a great local festival marked the arrival of the great altarpiece in the cathedral. Both sides are painted: on the front is the *Madonna enthroned between rows of Saints*, on the back, opposite the Majesty, the *Passion of Christ* is depicted in twenty-six compartments. In this rigorously divided work, the artist has succeeded admirably in blending highly-valued and sober Byzantine models with the new lyrical and human trend of the French Gothic style, creating an absolutely unique work in terms of the range of colours and the descriptive intensity. On the **second floor** we find a very ancient Sienese painting, the *Large-eyed Madonna* and works by Ambrogio Lorenzetti such as his *Four Saints*, as well as others by Simone Martini and Giovanni di Paolo.

Interior of the Baptistery with the baptismal font.

THE BAPTISTERY

The **Baptistery**, known also as the Parish Church of San Giovanni, is situated in the back part of the Cathedral. The fourteenth century façade is probably due to Domenico D'Agostino and was finished around 1382. Executed in white marble, it is divided into three by bands of small columns and marble decorations which frame the three large portals, the central one of which is surmounted by a cusp. The middle section of the façade is decorated with small hanging arches surmounted by three large pointed blind windows. The interior, finished under the direction of Camaino di Crescentino, is divided into three naves and dates back to 1325. The inner walls are frescoed with works by Vecchietta, Michele di Matteo from Bologna and Benvenuto di Giovanni, depicting the Apostles, the Sibyls and the Prophets, episodes from the Life of Jesus and The Miracles of Saint Anthony. The **baptismal font** is a fine example of a blend between Gothic refinement and Renaissance harmony. Placed on the two steps in the centre of the church, its base consists of a hexagonal-shaped basin surmounted by a pillar which supports the ciborium of the same shape. The **ciborium** and the statue of the Baptist above are by Jacopo della Quercia.

The basin is decorated with six bas-reliefs depicting important episodes in the life of the Baptist. Among these are the Annunciation of the birth of the Baptist, by Jacopo della Quercia, the Capture of the Baptist by Lorenzo Ghiberti (1427) and Herod's Feast by Donatello. The statues of the prophets in the niches of the ciborium are also by Jacopo della Quercia.

National Art Gallery: *Adoration of the Magi* - Bartolo di Fredi.

NATIONAL ART GALLERY

One of the most elegant late Gothic buildings in Siena, Palazzo Buonsignori is home to the **National Art Gallery**, a collection of works fundamental to our knowledge of Sienese painting from the 12th to the 17th century. The collection now numbers almost seven hundred paintings exhibited according to chronological and stylistic criteria in the thirty-eight rooms of the building. There follows a brief description of only some of the most interesting paintings on display in the Art Gallery: these include the *Madonna of the Franciscans* by Duccio di Buoninsegna, dated to around 1300. This priceless painting reveals a blend of the Byzantine tradition and the lyrical tone which foreshadows the Gothic style. Another masterpiece is the *Adoration of the Magi* by Bartolo di Fredi, finished between 1370 and 1380, remarkable for its vivid colours and structural layout.

There is an exquisite *Polyptych of Saint Dorothea* by Ambrogio Lorenzetto, executed towards 1332, which depicts at the centre the *Madonna and Child*, on the right *Saint Dorothea* and on the left *Saint Mary Magdalen*. Also by Ambrogio Lorenzetti is the splendid *Annunciation* of 1344, which reveals a new and more modern conception of perspective and magnifies the serene detachment of the Virgin faced with the revelation of the mystery. Also by Lorenzetti are the small panels which originate from the Municipal Archives and which represent *The City on* the *Sea and the Castle on the Lake shore*. These are the first paintings with an exclusively landscape subject in the whole of Europe, whose importance, setting aside their artistic value, is linked to their precise historical and descriptive value.

The splendid predella of 1436 is the work of Giovanni di Paolo: it depicts the *Flight into Egypt, the Presentation of Mary at the Temple* and the *Crucifixion*, paintings in which the artist, through his poetic art, succeeds admirably in incorporating the transcendental dimension into his depiction of reality. The decorative elegance of Pinturicchio, who spent a long time in Siena when he was commissioned to paint the frescoes for the Piccolomini Library, is magnificently represented here by the tondo which depicts the *Holy Family with San Giovannino*; the painting, which dates back to the time of the Umbrian painter's artistic maturity, originates from the Campansi Convent. On the other hand the *Christ at the column* by Giovanni Antonio Bazzi known as Sodoma, originates from the Convent of San Francesco and is a particularly refined and essential work. An important point of reference for Sienese painting of the fifteenth century can be seen in the *Last Supper* by Stefano di Giovanni known as Sassetta. The work was part of an altarpiece executed for the Wool Guild Chapel in Siena and recalls somewhat the style of Simone Martini and Pietro Lorenzetti, reinterpreted, however, with a totally new taste for colour and settings in perspective. For a long time the painting which depicts *Saint John in the desert*, dating back to 1436 and part of a triptych in the Basilica dell'Osservanza was attributed to Sassetta. Following a more careful study the work has been attributed to a master similar to Sassetta in terms of style and known as Maestro dell'Osservanza.

Flight into Egypt - Giovanni di Paolo.

Top: Holy Family - Pinturicchio.
Bottom: Christ at the Column - Sodoma.

SANCTUARY OF SAINT CATHERINE OF SIENA

In Via del Tiratoio stands the beautiful brick-built **house of Saint Catherine** with its double order of spacious loggias, the place where Caterina Benincasa lived (1347-1380), an active figure in exposing the dire necessity to modernize the Church by doing away with every political constraint, so that it may become free to pursue its mission of solidarity among mankind. Thanks to the extremely strong personality of this woman, Pope Gregory XI was persuaded to transfer the papal seat from Avignon back to Rome in 1337. The Saint was canonized in 1461 by Pope Pius II, while Pius XII proclaimed her joint patron saint of Italy together with Saint Francis of Assisi. After her canonization, Catherine's fellow citizens worked on the restoration and the consecration of her house, later transforming it into a Sanctuary. A number of alterations were carried out to the original structure of the house: in fact the lower oratory replaces what once used to be the laundry, the upper oratory stands in place of the kitchen, the oratory of the Crucifix has been set up in the vegetable garden and another oratory has been made out of the Saint's room. In the **upper oratory** the ceiling is decorated with gilded rosettes, while a painting by Bernardo Fungai represents *Saint Catherine with the stigmata*. Many other works decorate the oratory, including *Gregory XI returns to the papal seat in Rome* by Pomarancio, and in the lunette, the *Canonization of the Saint*, by Francesco Vanni. In the **oratory of the Saint's room**, the place in which Catherine prayed and received the eminent personalities of the age, the wall decoration is by Alessandro Franchi, who, in 1896, depicted *Seven Stories of the Saint*.

Sanctuary of Saint Catherine of Siena.

Basilica of San Domenico: Chapel of Saint Catherine.

Basilica of San Domenico: Chapel of Saint Catherine.

BASILICA OF SAN DOMENICO

The severe and magnificent Basilica dedicated to San Domenico, a massive red brick building, dominates the hill on which it stands. Begun in 1226 by the Dominican friars, the chosen design for the Basilica included a rectangular nave and an open truss-work roof. The façade remained unfinished.

The great **crypt** surmounted by wide cross vaults dates back to 1300 and thanks to the tombs which it contained was known as the Church Below or the Church of the Dead. The church houses works by Sodoma, Sano di Pietro and Turino di Sano. The bell-tower dates back to 1340 and its present reduced size is the result of works carried out in 1700. Inside the Basilica is the **Chapel of Saint Catherine**, which is entirely frescoed.

Among the most interesting scenes are T*he Ecstasy* and T*he swooning of the Saint* by Sodoma. On the altar is an elaborate marble tabernacle, the work of Giovanni di Stefano, in which the Saint's head is preserved. In the **Chapel of the Vaults** we can admire the only painting which faithfully reproduces the Saint's appearance: the *portrait of Saint Catherine* by Andrea Vanni.

The ciborium and the two delicate marble angels above the high altar in the Basilica are a work of 1475 by Benedetto da Maiano. The right-hand side of the façade provides access to the **cloister of San Domenico** dating back to 1425, where fresco fragments from the 14th century by Lippo Memmi and Andrea Vanni have been found.

BRANDA FOUNTAIN

It is the most famous one of the many fountains of Siena, already existing in 1081. It was later enlarged by Bellamino and remade in 1246 by Giovanni di Stefano. Probably it was so called after a nearby house belonging to a certain Brando or Ildebrando, or else after an old Brandi family.

It is made of bricks and has on its front three large ogive arches, surmounted by gables and adorned with merlons and four leonine gargolyes with the emblem of Siena in the middle. The fountain is dominated by the apse of the basilica of San Domenico.

The Branda Fountain and, in the background, the Basilica of San Domenico.

THE SIENA PALIO

The origins and the primitive character of the Siena Palio have never been satisfactorily explained. It is certain, however, that the city of Siena's most popular and exciting festival already existed well before 1310, the year when the official institution of the Palio was consecrated, to be competed for on the 16th August in honour of the Assumption into Heaven. It was after the victorious battle of Montaperti in 1260 that this popular feast took on an added political significance: the offering of candles since that time is meant to symbolize gratitude to the Madonna and the reaffirmation of the autonomy and independence of the Sienese Municipality. In 1656 the institution of a second Palio was officially recognized, the "Palio of the Districts", to be run on the 2nd July in honour of the Madonna of Provenzano. The Sienese Districts, which initially were fairly numerous, but later reduced to the seventeen we have today, are precise territorial organizations which gather together the citizens of the same neighbourhood. Their names are curious and symbolic: Tortoise, Wave, She-wolf, Shell, Goose, Porcupine, Dragon, Owl, Snail, Panther, Eagle, Caterpillar, Horned Lion, Vale of the Ram, Giraffe, Forest and Tower. Each District is supported by its own governmental organizations, elected every two years and whose existence hinges on the general assembly. Every Sienese lives the life of his District, which still plays a civil role in organizing its members' free time: as a result every occasion for a gathering is closely linked to a Sienese's particular District. For twelve months of the year the life of the District is in fervour, but during the days before the Palio the atmosphere becomes really explosive. Nowadays, as in the past, the event, and every aspect connected with it, involves the annual repetition of a rite. It begins with the blessing of the horse and the choice of rider (almost never a Sienese), a hero loved and hated, who passes down from generation to generation as a legend, to be regarded for the most part with suspicion. The historic Procession of the Districts follows, with standard bearers waving their flags, the insistent beat of the drums, and finally the arrival of the horses and the riders through the great entrance. The start of the race, known as the "mossa", is of fundamental importance. The horses line up between two hemp ropes according to the lots they have drawn: when the tenth and final horse has entered, the "rincorsa", the starter fires a device to signal that the tough and unpredictable race is on. In the three laps of the Campo anything can happen. The riders obstruct one another, hit each other, fall off, their bullwhips whirling in the air, some horses shake off their riders, but are not deterred from continuing their mad dash. Then follows triumph or defeat, singing, brawling, the blessing of the "cencio" (the rag, as the Sienese call the Palio), dinners and processions. There is no limit to the joy or the desperation felt after the race: the emotion lasts for days and leaves an indelible mark on every Sienese.

The festivities for the winning District include a Te Deum of thanksgiving at the Church of the Madonna of Provenzano on the 2nd July, in the Cathedral in August, and a magnificent Victory Dinner.

Index

TEXT: STEFANIA BELLONI

© Copyright
CASA EDITRICE PERSEUS
collection PLURIGRAF
Published and printed by
Centro Stampa Editoriale,
Sesto Fiorentino, (Fi).